W9-AQV-647

Date: 02/02/12

J 591.44 MIL
Miller, Sara Swan.
Mouths /

PALM BEACH COUNTY
LIBRARY SYSTEM
3650 SUMMIT BLVD.
WEST PALM BEACH, FL 33406

ALL KINDS OF MOUTHS

Sara Swan Miller

Marshall Cavendish
Benchmark
New York

Marshall Cavendish Benchmark
99 White Plains Road
Tarrytown, New York 10591-9001
www.marshallcavendish.us

Copyright © 2008 by Marshall Cavendish Corporation

All rights reserved. No part of this book may be reproduced or utilized in any form or by any means elec-
tronic or mechanical, including photocopying, recording, or by any information storage and retrieval system, without permission from the copyright holders.

All Web sites were available and accurate when this book was sent to press.

Editor: Doug Sanders
Publisher: Michelle Bisson
Art Director: Anahid Hamparian
Series Designer: Alex Ferrari

Library of Congress Cataloging-in-Publication Data

Miller, Sara Swan.
  Mouths / by Sara Swan Miller.
    p. cm. — (All kinds of ...)
  Summary: "An exploration of animal mouths, their various shapes and
functions"—Provided by publisher.
  Includes bibliographical references and index.
  ISBN-13: 978-0-7614-2521-2
  1. Mouth—Juvenile literature. I. Title. II. Series.

  QL857.M57 2007
  591.4'4—dc22

                          2006019711

Photo research by Anne Burns Images

Cover photo: Corbis/Denis Scott

The photographs in this book are used by permission and through the courtesy of: *Peter Arnold, Inc.:*
Norbert Wu, 2, 18; Hans Pfletschinger, 11, 12; BIOS, 29; Ed Reschke, 32; Paul Hicks, 34; Gerard Lacz, 41.
Corbis: Christine Schneider, 4; Visuals Unlimited, 7; Michael Keller, 9; Kevin Schafer, 10; Jeffrey L. Rotman,
14; Buddy Mays, 16; Lynda Richardson, 20; Fritz Rauschenbach/zefa, 22; Martin Harvey, 23; David A.
Northcott, 25; Michael & Patricia Fogden, 28 (top and bottom); Joe McDonald, 33; Dan Guravich, 36; Chris
Collins, 38; Theo Allofs/zefa, 42; Yann Arthus-Bertrand, 44. *Custom Medical Stock Photos:* 6. *Animals
Animals:* Zigmund Leszczynski, 17; Stephen Dalton, 26; ABPL/Nigel Dennis, 30; Mark Chappell, 35; Leonard
Rue Enterprises, 43; Alan G. Nelson, 45.

Printed in Malaysia
1 3 5 6 4 2

CONTENTS

This girl's new teeth are just beginning to grow in.

EVERYBODY HAS TO EAT

What is one thing all animals have in common? They all have to eat. Over millions and millions of years, animals have developed all kinds of mouths perfectly suited to the different foods they eat. Even the simplest animals have a mouth, although it may be just an opening that food can move through.

The human mouth, on the other hand, is very complex. Think of all the things you do with your mouth. Besides sucking, chewing, tasting, and swallowing, you also use your mouth to talk, smile, whistle, kiss, and even to breathe.

Our mouths house our teeth. In the course of our lives, we grow two sets. There are twenty teeth in the first set, sometimes called the milk teeth. When a person is around six years old, the milk teeth begin to be replaced by the permanent teeth. They push up from underneath. Usually by the time a person is seventeen, the permanent set of thirty-two teeth is complete. After that, if a tooth is lost, the body will never replace it.

We have four different kinds of teeth, which are suited to crunch, chew, and mash the various foods we eat.

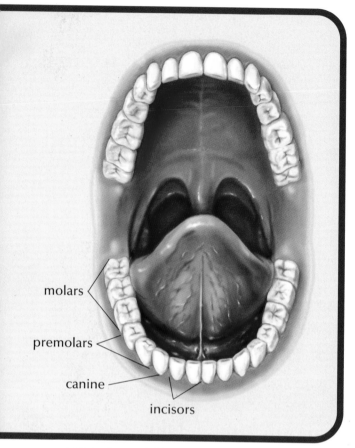

molars

premolars

canine

incisors

With four different kinds of teeth, human mouths are made for eating all types of food.

The front teeth, called the *incisors,* are nippers that cut the food. Behind them are the *canines,* which can grab and stab meat. Behind the canines are the *premolars,* then the *molars.* They both chew and grind the food before it is swallowed. People developed this tooth pattern long ago, so we know that early humans were omnivores, eating both plants and meat.

Your tongue is just as important in breaking down food. Without it, you would not be able to swallow, and you certainly would not be able to taste your food. Your tongue is a muscle that passes the food to your teeth, then pushes it down your throat. On the tongue's surface are little bumps called *papillae,* which make it rough. On the surface of the papillae are tiny taste buds that send taste signals to your brain.

Your taste buds can sense five basic tastes: sweet, sour, salty, bitter, and a recently named taste called umami, which is also referred to as savory. It is the taste found in *fermented* and aged foods, such as soy sauce or

A mammal tongue with its taste buds magnified many times.

THE NOSE KNOWS!

If you hold your nose and close your eyes, you can't taste the difference between an onion and an apple.

fish sauce. The taste buds near the front of your tongue are most sensitive to salty, sweet, and umami. The ones on the sides of your tongue are most sensitive to sour. The taste buds at the back of your tongue are most sensitive to bitter. If you can detect only five different tastes with your tongue, why do the various foods we eat each have their own taste? Most of your ability to taste actually comes from your sense of smell.

Besides eating, we also use our mouths to talk. In your throat is an organ called the larynx. It houses the vocal cords. These are bands of muscle covered with mucus. If you could look down your throat at your vocal cords, you would see that there are two. They join together to make a V. When you breathe in, the vocal cords are pulled apart, letting the air in. When you breathe out, the vocal cords close up. As you speak, muscles bring your vocal cords close together. When air passes through the closed cords, they vibrate and create sound.

Speaking, however, involves more than just making sounds. By changing the shape of your mouth and moving your tongue and lips into various positions, you can form many different sounds and words. We usually talk without thinking about what our mouths are doing. Try saying this sentence slowly and out loud: "People use

Think of how hard it would be to express yourself, if you didn't have a mouth.

their mouths to talk." Pay attention to what your tongue and lips are doing when you make each sound and how your mouth cavity changes shape. Human speech is incredibly complex.

Animals may not be able to talk, but they use their mouths in a variety of ways. There are all kinds of different mouths in the animal kingdom. Some are a lot like ours, and some are completely different. There are sucking mouths, biting mouths, chewing mouths, lapping mouths, and gulping mouths, to name just a few. Each kind of animal has developed a mouth perfectly suited to the foods it eats and the place where it lives.

This morpho butterfly has curled up its tongue.

INCREDIBLE INSECT MOUTHS

Insects have developed a fascinating variety of mouth-parts. Whatever there is to eat, an insect has adapted or changed to be able to eat it. Insect foods include all kinds of plants, pollen, nectar, other insects, worms, rotting meat, flakes of dead skin, blood, and even animal droppings.

STAG WARS

Stag beetles have huge *mandibles*. They look as though they could give you a sharp bite. But a stag beetle's mandibles are actually rather weak. If you pick this insect up, it may give you a tiny nip. Male stag beetles use their mandibles to battle each other to see who will win a female. They lock their mandibles together and push each other back and forth until one of them gives up.

A male stag beetle has huge mandibles.

Many insects have a mouth suited for biting and breaking up tough food. Their large mandibles act like scissors. Behind the mandibles is a pair of *maxillae*, which are like a back-up pair of jaws. They help hold and break up food. Ants, beetles, cockroaches, dragonflies, and grasshoppers all have biting mouthparts. Insects that eat meat, such as ground beetles and praying mantises, have much bigger mandibles than the ones used only to clip and chew leaves.

Many other insects have mouthparts used for sucking. Cicadas, aphids, butterflies, moths, and the *true bugs* all suck up their food. Some true bugs, such as bedbugs, draw in blood with their long beak. Others, such as chinch bugs and stink bugs, take in plant juices. Another true bug, the water boatman, uses its soft beak to gather ooze from the bottom of a

A pine hawkmoth caterpillar chews on a stem.

pond. Moths and butterflies have mouths that are specially adapted for sucking nectar. They have extra long tongues they can unroll and stick deep into a flower where the nectar is hidden.

MOUTH METAMORPHOSIS

A caterpillar has mouthparts good for chewing up leaves. As it turns into a moth or butterfly, its mouth becomes a curled-up straw.

There are still other types of mouths found in the insect world. A female mosquito, for instance, sucks mammal or bird blood to help feed her eggs. Her mouth has six sharp needlelike parts that are perfect for drawing blood. The mosquito uses four of the needles to slice into the skin of the host. The insect then presses the other two needles together to make a tube that sucks up the blood. A house fly, on the other hand, has no piercing mouthparts. To eat, it vomits digestive juices on its food, then laps up the dissolved juice.

Some adult insects, such as mayflies, actually don't eat at all. The young, which live in streams or ponds, take in small pieces of plant and animal material using their biting mouthparts. Once they emerge from the water, the adults live only a short time—sometimes just a few hours. Their only job is to mate and lay eggs. There is just no time to eat too!

*A bluetail trunkfish has big
fleshy lips.*

3

FABULOUS FISH MOUTHS

Fish mouths are perfectly suited for living and feeding in the water. Fish have tongues and jaws that move up and down much the way ours do. Most fish have teeth as well.

Many fishes have a mouth shaped like a cone. They have a fairly small mouth opening and a rear section that can expand or grow in size. When a fish suddenly expands the back of its mouth, water comes rushing in, bringing a mouthful of food with it. This kind of mouth is perfect for sucking in a lot of small prey at the same time. That way some fish can draw in more food at one time than if they had to grab and bite their prey one by one.

Fishes that capture large prey, such as barracudas and bluefish, have a large mouth opening and a mouth cavity shaped like a cylinder. These kinds of fishes cannot feed

PLENTY OF TEETH

If you dared to look inside a shark's mouth, you would see several rows of teeth lined up side by side. In the front row are the teeth it currently uses to catch its prey. The ones behind the front teeth are replacements. When a shark loses a front tooth, a new one moves forward to take its place.

A needle-nosed gar has a lot of very sharp teeth.

by sucking in their food. Instead, they swim swiftly toward their prey, open their mouths wide, and gulp it down. This is called ram feeding.

A fish's teeth are adapted to the kinds of food it eats. Fishes that eat mostly other fish, such as pike and gars, have sharp, pointed teeth. They use them for grasping, spearing, and holding their prey. Fishes such as skates and drums that feed on snails, crabs, and other hard-bodied creatures have grinding teeth. Those that feed on plant matter, such as parrot fish, have sharp-edged ridges on their jaws. The ridges are formed by the joining of individual teeth. They chop up their food into a kind of salad. Fishes that feed on *plankton*—tiny creatures that float in the water—are usually toothless. There's nothing to chew!

Some fishes, such as lampreys, have no jaws. Their mouth is a round disk full of sharp "teeth." Inside is a toothed "piston." To feed on a live fish, a lamprey first attaches itself to its prey. Then it rocks its piston back and forth, sawing away at the flesh.

From its name, you would think that an elephantnose fish had a nose like an elephant's. What it really has is a

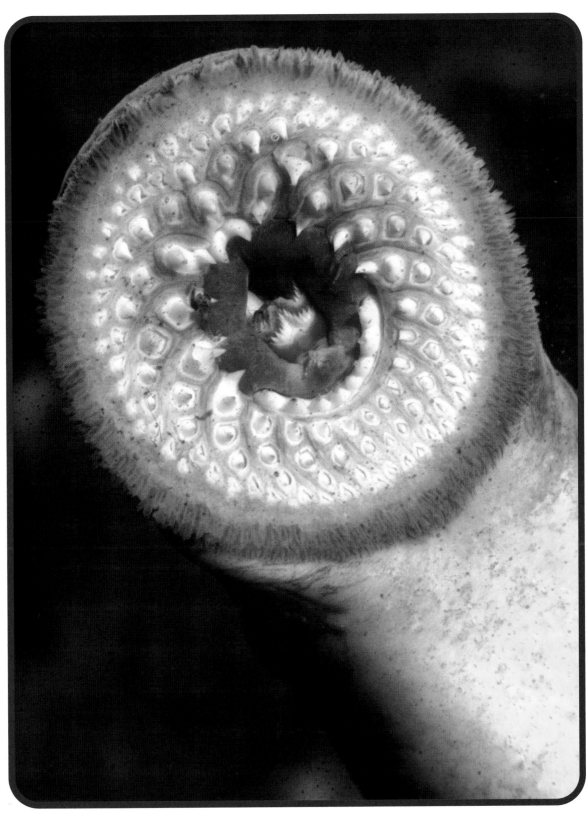

A sea lamprey fastens onto its prey with its sucker-like mouth.

A PLUCKY EATER

A long-nose butterfly fish swims among coral and sea urchins, using its jaws like tweezers to pluck out its food.

very long chin. As it swims slowly along, it uses its long chin to search the muddy bottom for food.

One look at a sailfish's sword-like beak and you know it means business. That sharp sword is really a long upper jaw. A sailfish swims at high speed through a school of fish, slashing with its sword and injuring its prey. Then it quickly turns and swallows its meal.

An American paddlefish has a unique mouth as well. Inside there are flabby gills and tiny teeth. Its top "lip" is

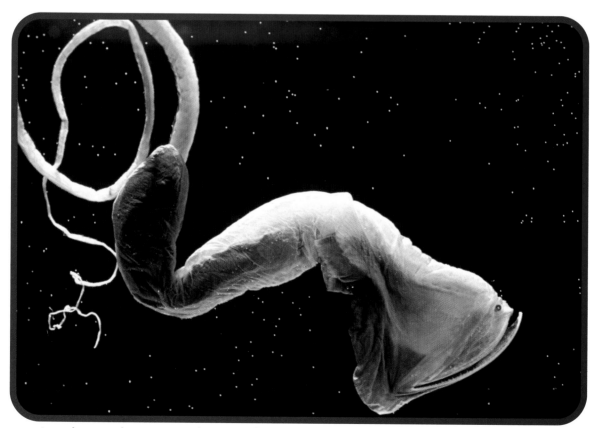

A gulper eel seems to be mostly mouth.

long and shaped like a paddle. As it swims along, the fish uses its paddle to sense the plankton it feeds on. It swims through the plankton with its mouth gaping wide, straining the bits of food through its gills.

Sea horses and pipefishes have mouths unlike most other kinds of fishes. Instead of large jaws that they can open and close, they have long, thin tube-shaped mouths. They use their mouths like vacuum cleaners to suck up tiny animals in the water.

When it comes to mouth sizes, the gulper eel is at the other extreme. It has a huge mouth. Its jaws make up nearly one-fourth of its body length. A gulper eel lives deep in the sea. With its enormous mouth opened wide, it takes in loads of tiny shrimp. The gulper eel is certainly well named!

The mouth of a spotted salamander is filled with tiny teeth.

AWESOME AMPHIBIAN AND REPTILE MOUTHS

If you could look inside the mouth of a land salamander, the first things you might notice are the tiny teeth on its jaws and on the roof of its mouth. A salamander doesn't use its teeth for chewing food as we do. Mostly they are for holding and pinning down a salamander's prey until it can be swallowed.

Land salamanders have well-developed and flexible tongues. Sticky mucus on the surface helps them grab and hold their insect prey. A few salamanders use their tongues the way some frogs do. Some lungless salamanders, for instance, shoot out their sticky mushroom-shaped tongues to catch prey that is passing by.

Salamanders that spend most of their lives in the water have much simpler tongues. They are no more than fleshy folds on the floor of the mouth. Because the tongue has no muscles, a salamander that lives in the water can't move its tongue and use it to help catch prey. The salamander just opens its wide mouth to grab a small passing fish or a water insect. Then it gulps its meal.

TOOTHLESS TOADS

Unlike frogs, toads have no teeth at all. They just gulp their food whole.

Do frogs have teeth? They certainly do, but their tiny teeth are hard to see. Frogs have a ridge of small cone-shaped teeth around the edge of their upper jaws. But they have no teeth on the bottom jaw. Usually, frogs swallow their prey whole. So their tiny teeth are no good for chewing, just for holding prey in place.

When it comes to catching prey, a frog or toad's most important organ is its tongue. Most frogs and toads have a long, sticky tongue that is attached in the front of the mouth and free at the back. Their long tongue is

A frog can snag insects with its long, sticky tongue.

very sticky. When an insect flies by, some frogs can flick out their tongues in an instant and snag their prey. It happens so fast that you might not even see it.

Most male frogs are incredibly noisy in the spring when they are calling to their mates. They force air from their lungs through their larynx, which makes their vocal cords vibrate and so create sounds. These frogs can make an incredible racket for such small animals. What makes their calls so loud? Most male frogs have one or more vocal sacs, pouches of skin on their throat or at the corners of their mouth. When air is forced through the sacs from the larynx, they act like a rock band's amplifiers, turning up the sound. Each species of frog has its own call, which the females can easily recognize.

What would you find inside a turtle's mouth? You certainly wouldn't find any teeth. Then how do turtles eat? Most have tough, horny ridges covering their upper and lower jaws. Their mouth is somewhat like a

A giant tortoise has a horny beak instead of teeth.

EYEWASH

Geckos cannot close their eyes. To keep them clean and moist, geckos lick their eyes with their tongues.

bird's bill. Meat-eating turtles, such as snapping turtles, have knife-like ridges that can tear into prey. Plant eaters, such as tortoises, have serrated or jagged edges on their jaw ridges. That makes it easy for them to bite off pieces of hard, woody plants.

Turtles may be toothless, but they do have tongues. Most turtles use their tongues just to help them swallow. An alligator snapping turtle, however, has another use for its tongue. On the tip of it is a pink, fleshy "lure." The turtle lies still on the pond bottom with its mouth open, waving the lure back and forth. It looks like a worm wiggling in the water. When a fish swims up hoping for a juicy meal, the snapper snaps it up.

Most lizards are *carnivores*. They have jaws full of sharp teeth. The huge monitor lizards have especially efficient teeth. Their large teeth curve backward and have serrated or saw-like edges. With them, they can slice into the meat of large prey, including deer and water buffalo.

Lizards have all kinds of tongues. Some have long, slender forked tongues, like snakes' tongues. When beaded lizards, monitor lizards, and legless slow worms flick their tongues out of their mouths, they can pick up smells and chemicals with it that will lead them to their prey. Geckos and flap foot lizards have a fleshy tongue that they use to lap up water or nectar.

Some lizards, such as the blue-tongued skink, have brightly colored tongues. What good is a bright blue tongue? When the skink is scared, it puffs itself up, hisses, and sticks out its huge flashy tongue. That is usually all that is needed to scare away a predator.

This blue-tongued skink is trying to scare off an intruder with its flashy tongue.

Do lizards have venom? Only one kind does—the beaded lizards. They have venom glands in their bottom jaws. The gila monster is a large beaded lizard that can deliver a painful bite if you get too close. Although a gila monster's bite would hurt, it probably wouldn't kill you.

Unlike lizards, many snakes are venomous, especially tropical snakes. They have venom glands and fangs in the front or rear of their upper jaws. When a snake bites into its prey, muscles in its jaws release the venom through the hollow fangs. Usually, a poisonous snake uses its venom only to stun or kill its prey, but some snakes also bite in self-defense.

Some venomous snakes, such as cobras, have fixed fangs that are attached firmly to the jawbone. Since

INCREDIBLE CHAMELEONS

A chameleon has an incredibly long tongue that it uses to catch prey. On the tip is a sticky pouch, while at its base the tongue is attached to a bone. By squeezing the tongue muscles against the bone, a chameleon can shoot its tongue out with amazing speed and snag its prey using the sticky tip. This works somewhat like squeezing a wet bar of soap to shoot it out of your hand. A chameleon can extend its tongue so fast that it takes only $1/100$ of a second to catch an insect—faster than the eye can see. A chameleon can grab an insect from a long distance, because its tongue may be longer than its body. It also has a flexible body that can stretch to great lengths, while the chameleon holds on with its *prehensile* tail. When a chameleon is not eating, it keeps its tongue bunched up in its mouth. What a mouthful!

With its long, sticky tongue, a veiled chameleon can catch a cricket that is several inches away.

these snakes need to be able to close their mouths, their fangs cannot be too long. Other venomous snakes, including many vipers, have long folding fangs. When these snakes strike, the fangs swing forward. When the snakes close their mouths, their fangs curl back inside.

DANGER!
Australia's inland taipan snake is deadly. A single bite can contain enough venom to kill 250,000 mice.

Snakes' mouths are small compared to the rest of their bodies. So how do they get enough to eat? One solution is to eat a variety of small creatures. Wormsnakes, for instance, eat large amounts of worms and insect larvae. Other snakes catch larger prey and tear off pieces small enough to swallow.

Yet another solution is having special flexible jaws. Many snakes have lower jaws that are not fused together. Instead, the two halves are joined at the front by an elastic part called a ligament. These snakes also have special bones linking the lower jaws to the skull. These adaptations mean that the snakes can open their mouths incredibly wide and swallow prey much larger than the size of their own heads.

One amazing example is the egg-eating snake of Africa. It feeds on bird eggs, many of them so much larger than its own mouth that you wonder how the snake is able to swallow them. Inside its mouth are folds that act like suction cups and hold onto the slippery egg. Once the snake has managed to get the whole egg into its

An egg-eater snake can swallow an egg much bigger than its head.

mouth and swallow it, spines in its neck pierce the shell. The yolk and the liquids inside then run down the snake's throat. Later, the snake throws up the crushed bits of leftover shell.

Snakes are always flicking their long forked tongues in and out of their mouths. Are they trying to scare you? No, they're just tasting and smelling. The tongue picks up tiny particles in the air, then funnels them to the *Jacobson's organ* on the roof of the mouth. The Jacobson's organ can sort out different smells and tastes, so the snake knows what kind of prey and predators are around.

One look at an alligator's gaping jaws and big teeth will tell you that it is definitely not a vegetarian. In the water, it gobbles up

A Nile crocodile opens wide.

fish, turtles, and frogs. When it goes on land, it uses its big head to smash through plants and ground cover as its chases after mammals, snakes, and even birds.

Alligators and crocodiles have mouths specially adapted to hunting in the water. When they open their mouths underwater to grab a fish, they close off the back of the throat with a fleshy valve found at the base of the tongue. That way, they can eat underwater without drowning.

This ground hornbill needs strong muscles in order to hold up its heavy bill.

BEAUTIFUL BIRD BILLS

Everything about a bird is designed for flying, even its mouth. If a bird had a mouth like a mammal's, with its heavy jaws and teeth, it would just weigh the bird down. Instead, birds have bills, which are light yet strong. A bird's bill has a bony shell on the inside, covered with a thin outer plate of *keratin*. This is the same material that your fingernails are made of.

You can get a good idea of what a bird eats by looking at its bill. A seed eater, such as a cardinal, has a large crushing bill. Insect eaters usually have narrow, tweezer-like bills. Woodpeckers' bills are like chisels, excellent for drilling into trees in search of insects. Wading birds, such as snipes, have long bills that they use for poking and probing in the water for food. The tips of their bills are very sensitive and allow snipes to feel their prey hiding in the mud. Birds such as the oystercatcher, which feeds on mussels and limpets, have a strong, blunt hammer bill, good for prying open the hard shells.

Geese and ducks have broad bills. Geese use them to tear off the grass they eat. Ducks use their bills for what is called dabbling. As they swim, they open and close their bills on the surface. As water enters, the bill strains out the bits of food floating in it.

Raptors—birds that hunt rodents, birds, and other small animals—have strong hooked bills. Owls and hawks, for instance, use their sharp bills to tear up their prey.

Fish eaters have bills that are well adapted to catching their fast-moving meals. A heron, for example, uses its long, tapered beak to spear and grasp its prey. A cormorant, on the other hand, has a long, slender bill with a hook on the end. The hook helps it grab slippery fish as it dives underwater. A merganser has a different way of catching fish. Along the sides of its bill are little notches, almost like teeth, that help it grab and hold its prey.

Some birds have bills that are designed for eating more than one kind of food. A parrot feeds on both fruit and seeds. It uses the hook on the tip of its bill to tear up fruit, but it crushes up seeds with the large jaws at the base of its bill. Crows have strong,

A military macaw can feed on both fruit and seeds.

all-purpose bills. One reason crows thrive is that they can eat just about anything. Insects, rodents, worms, seeds, garbage, dead animals—you name it and a crow will most likely eat it.

A toucan has a large, colorful bill, so large that the bird looks as though it is all bill. How can a toucan fly with *that* on its face? Actually, a toucan's bill is not as heavy as it looks. Although the outside is hard and horny, the inside is hollow. Bony rods crisscross to help support the bill. A toucan's bill is an ideal tool for plucking fruits and berries growing on the tips of twigs. The heavy toucan could never get to that fruit without the help of its huge bill.

Hornbills also have extra-large bills. Their heavy

SHOE FACE

The aptly named shoebill stork looks as though it is wearing a Dutch clog, a thick wooden shoe, on its face.

The well-named whale-headed stork is also called a shoebill.

heads are held up by strong neck muscles. Their first two neck vertebrae, part of their backbones, are fused for added strength. Many species, including the great Indian hornbill, have big *casques* on the tops of their bills. The casques act as ridges running along the top of the head and giving it added strength. Great Indian hornbills, like some other hornbills, use their hollow casque to help amplify and increase the sound of their loud, roaring calls.

A puffin's large colorful bill makes it look like a little clown. But this bird is a serious hunter. It dives deep underwater to catch fish in its bill. A puffin can hold up to thirty wiggling fish in its bill at once.

A pelican may look strange, with a big pouch hanging under its bill, but that pouch is great for fishing. A pelican flies over the water, peering into the depths below. When it spots a fish, the pelican suddenly veers, turns, and dives headfirst into the water. In a few seconds it rises to the surface with a fish in its pouch. Then it flings back its head and gulps the fish whole. Some people think a

An arctic puffin's showy bill can hold a lot of fish at once.

pelican stores food in its pouch, but no pelican could fly with its pouch full of heavy fish.

A flamingo uses its bill to feed in a unique way. The bird walks through the water with its head down, dipping its bill upside down in the water. The bill acts like a sieve to strain out small animals and plants living in the water. The lower bill moves up and down, pumping out the water. The upper bill has a fringe of slits that trap the food bits.

It is obvious how a spoonbill gets its name. Its bill is shaped like a spoon, a great tool for feeding on fish, shrimp, crabs, and other small water creatures. As a spoonbill wades through the water, it sweeps its partly open

USEFUL BILLS

Birds use their bills for more than just eating, because they can't use their forelegs the way other animals can. Since wings replace what would have been the front legs, birds have to do most things with their bills. Birds use their bills to clean their feathers, fight with rivals, and gather nesting material.

A brown pelican uses its bill to preen its feathers.

bill back and forth below the surface. When the bird feels a tasty creature with its bill's sensitive tip, the bill snaps shut.

A skimmer is another bird with a unique bill. The lower part is much longer than the upper part. This allows the skimmer to fly just over the surface, plowing the water with its long lower mandible. The instant a skimmer feels a fish, it snaps its bill shut and flies off with its catch.

No bird has teeth, but they all have tongues. Bird tongues come in all shapes. They may be cylindrical, rectangular, spoon shaped, flat, or tube-like. Different birds use their tongues in different ways. Their tongues can act as probes, brushes, sieves, straws, or saws.

Woodpeckers have a long, slender tongue—longer

A black skimmer's lower bill is longer than its upper bill.

BIRDS WITHOUT TASTE
Birds don't have much of a sense of taste. Most have only twenty-five to seventy taste buds.

than any other bird's. They can insert their barbed, sticky tongues deep into tree holes they have drilled in order to pick up insects hiding inside. Where does a woodpecker store that long tongue? Believe it or not, its tongue wraps around the top of its skull, under the skin, when it isn't feeding. The tongue is anchored inside the right nostril, then goes up between the eyes, over the top of the skull, down the back of the skull, and finally out through the bill.

Birds also use their mouths to communicate with one another. Instead of a larynx like a mammal's, birds have a *syrinx*. It is found in the throat where the windpipe branches. When a bird forces air through the syrinx, it causes thin membranes to vibrate. A syrinx is more efficient and complex than our larynx. A bird can create sound with almost all the air that passes through the syrinx. Our larynx uses only 2 percent of the air we exhale. A bird's syrinx can also create two separate sounds at the same time. How can that be? The syrinx sits on two separate breathing tubes, each side with its own membranes. That is how thrushes create their beautiful two-tone songs.

Like other predators, this dog has a full set of meat-eating teeth.

6

MARVELOUS MAMMAL MOUTHS

Mammals have many different types of teeth, each with its own special function. Incisors, which are in the front of a mammal's mouth, are good for biting and nipping. Canine teeth, which come next, are good for tearing meat. The premolars, along with the larger molars behind them, help grind and chew food.

Not every mammal has all these types of teeth, though. You can tell a lot about what a mammal eats by looking at what kinds of teeth it has.

Predators that live on land, including wolves, badgers, skunks, dogs, and cats, have a full set of teeth. They are adapted to eating meat. A predator's incisors are sharp, and its canine teeth are large and pointed. Like fangs, they help the predator keep a good grip on its prey. Behind the canines are *carnassial teeth*—one on each side on the bottom and on the top. These teeth are good for tearing meat. Strong molars at the rear then help the predator chew up the pieces.

Mammals that eat grass and plants, such as horses, have very different teeth. A horse has large incisors that

A USEFUL GAP
The gap between a horse's front and back teeth is where people put the bit they use when riding and guiding the animal.

it uses to tear off grass. Then it grinds the grass with its big, ridged molars. Horses have no canine teeth, though. They don't need them. So between the incisors and the molars, where canine teeth would otherwise be, there is just a gap.

A white-tailed deer, which eats grasses, leaves, and twigs, has teeth a lot like a horse's. But it has no upper incisors or upper canines. Instead, there is a leathery pad. When the deer tears off a branch, it presses its bottom incisors against the pad and pulls. Most other deer have teeth like a white-tailed deer, but two species are a little different. The musk deer of Asia and the Chinese water deer have two sharp tusks on their upper jaw. Unlike other deer species, the males have no antlers with which to fight over the females. So these males spar with their tusks, instead.

Rodents such as mice, chipmunks, and muskrats eat mostly plant matter. They have large, chisel-like incisors good for gnawing and nipping. The incisors are coated with hard enamel in the front, but the back is softer. When a rodent gnaws, the back of the incisor wears down faster than the front. That keeps the incisors very sharp. With all the gnawing a rodent does, its incisors wear down quickly. But that is never a problem. A rodent's incisors keep growing throughout its life. Behind the incisors is a gap, where the rodent's canine teeth would have been. Then come the molars, good for chewing plants.

How about shrews and moles? Do they have teeth like rodents? Shrews and moles are insect eaters, so their teeth are very different. They have a full set of sharp teeth, including pointed canine teeth, which are excellent for tearing up prey.

Some mammals do not have many teeth at all. Armadillos, for instance, have just a few cylindrical teeth in the back of their jaws. Armadillos feed on ants, so they don't really need a lot of teeth. They just grind the ants a little bit before swallowing them.

Some mammals don't have any teeth. An anteater, for example, has a long, slender snout and a long tongue it uses to probe for ants. But it doesn't need teeth. It just swallows the ants whole and digests them in its stomach. A platypus is another toothless mammal. Inside its leathery, duck-like bill it has grinding pads instead of teeth. When it gathers worms, shellfish, and insects for its dinner, it also scoops up gravel. As it grinds its food between the

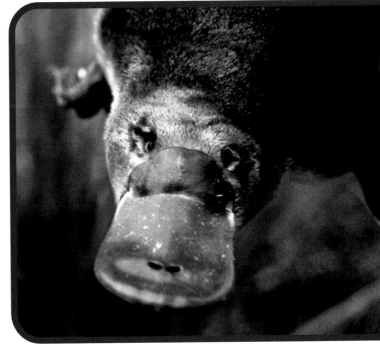

A platypus has leathery pads inside its bill instead of teeth.

A MOUTH LIKE A SIEVE

A baleen whale has a unique system for eating. Instead of teeth, it has comb-like plates called *baleen* in its upper jaw. As the whale swims, it takes in mouthfuls of water filled with small fish and shrimp-like krill. The baleen acts like a strainer. The whale pushes its tongue against the baleen, and the water rushes out. The food, however, stays behind, trapped by the baleen. Then the whale gulps it down.

leathery pads, the gravel helps crush its meal.

Some mammals have tusks. When you think of tusks, what is the first mammal that comes to mind? You probably picture an elephant. An elephant's tusks are really just long, upcurved incisors. The males use their tusks to battle over the females. But elephants also use their tusks as tools. Tusks are good for prying bark off trees or for uprooting a bush so the elephant can gnaw on the roots.

Some hogs also have tusks. A warthog has four curved tusks, which are really just long canine teeth. The sharp tusks are great for defending itself against lions and other predators. A babirusa is another type of wild hog. It has two long lower tusks and two even longer ones that grow

A warthog's sharp tusks help the animal protect itself.

through the top of its snout. It uses the lower ones to defend itself, but the top ones seem completely useless. They curve backward and sometimes even grow in a circle. They may, however, help males

Walrus tusks can grow very long.

attract a mate. The longer and curvier a male's tusks are, the more a female will be interested in him.

The first things you notice about a walrus are the incredibly long tusks growing from its upper jaw. They are actually canine teeth, and both male and female walruses have them. Males use their tusks to fight with one another over females. Both sexes use their tusks to fight off polar bears and other predators. Tusks also help a heavy walrus climb out of the water. It hooks them on a chunk of ice and hauls itself out.

The narwhal is sometimes called "the unicorn of the sea." The male has a single, long spiraling tusk sticking out from the tip of his snout. Females are attracted to this tusk—the longer the better. A narwhal's tusk may grow up to 8 feet (244 centimeters) long.

All mammals have tongues. They use their tongues for tasting their food, and for guiding it to the back of their mouths and swallowing it. Many mammals, particularly cats, use their tongues to clean their fur. Others, including dogs, use their tongues to cool off. A dog doesn't have cooling sweat glands all over its body the way we do. Instead, when it gets hot, a dog opens its mouth and pants.

Some mammals have tongues that are specially adapted for their diet. A porpoise, for instance, eats fish but has a small mouth. So it moves its tongue back and forth like a piston, creating suction so it can draw in its fish prey.

A giraffe's long, flexible tongue helps it grab leaves.

Giraffes and their cousins the okapis feed on leaves. Both have long, flexible tongues that can wrap around leaves high in a tree and pull them off.

Some mammals have tongues adapted for feeding on nectar. A fruit-eating bat, for instance, has a long snout and a tongue that it can stick deep into a flower to reach the nectar. A fruit-eating bat's tongue is one-third the length of its body. A honey possum is an Australian animal that gathers both nectar and pollen from flowers. The nectar and pollen stick to bristles on the end of its long, thin tongue.

Other mammals, such as aardvarks and anteaters, have tongues perfect for eating ants and termites. Both have long, sticky tongues that can reach far inside an ant nest or a termite mound. They catch thousands of ants and termites a day.

A few mammals have special mouths adapted to their unique habitats. A naked mole rat, for instance, lives its whole life underground tunneling through the dirt. It uses its huge incisors like chisels. So why doesn't it get dirt in its mouth? While it digs, its lips close behind the incisors and block any dirt from getting inside.

FAST TONGUES

An anteater can flick its tongue in and out of a termite nest as many as 160 times a minute.

The collared anteater has a very long tongue.

Another rodent, the beaver, lives mostly in the water, but it has a mouth a lot like the mole rat's. When it dives underwater, flaps of skin close behind its incisors. That way, it can chew underwater without getting a mouthful of water.

Mammal mouths are marvelous. All animal mouths, whether it is a bird bill or a reptile's tooth-lined jaws, are essential for survival. Mouths help with eating, communicating, mating, and almost everything animals do.

GLOSSARY

baleen—Comblike bristles in a baleen whale's mouth used for straining food.

canine—A tooth behind the incisors used for cutting.

carnassial tooth—A carnivore's tooth behind the canine tooth used for tearing meat.

carnivore—A flesh-eating animal.

casque—A helmet-like structure on some birds' bills.

fermented—Aged through the addition of another substance that changes the makeup of a food or beverage.

incisor—A front tooth used for nipping.

Jacobson's organ—An organ on the roof of a snake's mouth that can detect different smells and tastes. Other animals have them too.

keratin—The material that fingernails and the outer plate of bird bills are made of.

mandible—The part of some insects' jaws that cuts or slices food.

maxilla—The part of some insects' mouths under the mandible that acts like backup jaws.

molar—A tooth at the back of the jaw used for chewing and grinding.

papilla—A small bump on the surface of the tongue that houses taste buds.

plankton—Tiny animal and plant life floating in the water.

prehensile—Able to curl and grip around objects, as in a flexible tail.

premolar—A tooth behind the canine teeth used for chewing and grinding.

syrinx—An organ in a bird's throat that creates sound.

true bug—A member of an order of insects that have sucking mouthparts and wings that are half hard and half membrane.

FIND OUT MORE

BOOKS

Barre, Michel. *Animal Senses*. Milwaukee, WI: Gareth Stevens, 1998.

Berger, Melvin. *Flies Taste with Their Feet: Weird Facts about Insects*. New York: Scholastic, 1997.

Cerfolli, Fulvio. *Adapting to the Environment*. Austin, TX: Raintree Steck-Vaughn, 1999.

Grambo, Rebecca L. *Claws and Jaws*. Vero Beach, FL: Rourke, 2001.

Hickman, Pamela, and Pat Stephens. *Animal Senses: How Animals See, Hear, Taste, Smell, and Feel*. Buffalo, NY: Kids Can Press, 1998.

Kalman, Bobbie. *How Do Animals Adapt?* New York: Crabtree, 2000.

Parker, Steve. *Adaptation*. Chicago, IL: Heinemann Library, 2002.

Savage, Stephen. *Mouths*. New York: Thompson Learning, 1995.

Viegas, Jennifer. *The Mouth and Nose: Learning How We Taste and Smell*. New York: Rosen, 2001.

ORGANIZATIONS AND WEB SITES

The Animal Diversity Web
http://animaldiversity.ummz.umich.edu/
This site contains information about individual species in several different classes of animals, particularly mammals.

The Audubon Society
http://www.audubon.org
This organization is an amazing source of information for people interested in birds and bird watching.

Insect Inspecta World
http://www.insecta-inspecta.com
This site has all kinds of information about insects.

Neuroscience for Kids—Amazing Animal Senses
http://faculty.washington.edu/chudler/amaze.html
At this site you can learn a lot of amazing facts about animal senses.

INDEX

Page numbers for illustrations are in **boldface**.

ABOUT THE AUTHOR

Sara Swan Miller has enjoyed working with children all her life, first as a Montessori nursery school teacher and later as an outdoor environmental educator at the Mohonk Preserve in New Paltz, New York. As director of the school program, she has taught hundreds of children the importance of appreciating the natural world.

She has written more than fifty books, including *Three Stories You Can Read to Your Dog; Three Stories You Can Read to Your Cat; Three More Stories You Can Read to Your Dog; Three More Stories You Can Read to Your Cat; Three Stories You Can Read to Your Teddy Bear; Will You Sting Me? Will You Bite? The Truth about Some Scary-looking Insects;* and *What's in the Woods? An Outdoor Activity Book.* She has also written many nonfiction books for children.